ENDORSEMENTS

"As the parish priest of his youth, and now as his friend in adulthood, I can happily testify that Ed's joy and enthusiasm is as rich now as it was then. God sends people into our lives as His messengers. I assure you that Ed in person is as full of divine love and hope as is his writing. If you want a reminder of the goodness of life, of human beings, and of God, read this book. Ed is contagious. He is a gift from God. He enriches my spirit."

Father Neil Conway

"I have known Ed for over twenty years and have read the draft copy of Keys to Glory. It is a riveting story that holds your attention from beginning to end. There are times during Ed's story that you will wonder if he will find God. Pick up the book and I guarantee you that you cannot set it down until you finish and see how things turn out."

Thomas J. Malkus
Retired President, Data Processing Sciences, and friend

Ed shares two delightful gifts with us in his book. Not only are we introduced to his story, his growing up years in Cleveland, his religious training, and his love for music. We are also introduced to His story, the story of how God pursues a young man and wins his heart. Read this book. You will enjoy it, and you may even find your own key to glory.

Chris Martin
Senior Pastor–Linworth Road
Community Church Columbus, OH

"I found Ed's book to be an entertaining, yet straightforward story of his journey to Jesus. You'll be blessed as I was."

Bob Burney
Host - Bob Burney Live!
WRFD Radio
Columbus, Ohio
CrossPower Ministries

Keys to
GLORY

Steve!

*Praise Him w/
stringed instruments
Psalm 150:4*

Ed Bottacker

Edward T. Rothacker

KEYS TO

GLORY

A Catholic's *Search* for God

Tate Publishing & *Enterprises*

Keys to Glory—A Catholic's Search for God
Copyright © 2008 by Edward T. Rothacker. All rights reserved.

This title is also available as a Tate Out Loud product. Visit www.tatepublishing.com for more information.

No part of this publication may be reproduced, stored in a retrieval system or transmitted in any way by any means, electronic, mechanical, photocopy, recording or otherwise without the prior permission of the author except as provided by USA copyright law.

Scripture quotations marked "NAS" are taken from the New American Standard Bible ®, Copyright © 1960, 1962, 1963, 1968, 1971, 1972, 1973, 1975, 1977, 1995 by The Lockman Foundation. Used by permission. All rights reserved.

The opinions expressed by the author are not necessarily those of Tate Publishing, LLC.

Published by Tate Publishing & Enterprises, LLC
127 E. Trade Center Terrace | Mustang, Oklahoma 73064 USA
1.888.361.9473 | www.tatepublishing.com

Tate Publishing is committed to excellence in the publishing industry. The company reflects the philosophy established by the founders, based on Psalm 68:11,
"The Lord gave the word and great was the company of those who published it."

Book design copyright © 2008 by Tate Publishing, LLC. All rights reserved.
Cover design by Jacob Crissup
Interior design by Joey Garrett

Published in the United States of America

ISBN: 978-1-60604-156-7
1. Christian Living: Practical Life: Personal Growth
2. Biography & Autobiography: Composers & Musicians: General/Religious
08.04.25

TABLE OF CONTENTS

9	Foreword
11	A West Side Story
15	First Step Toward God
17	A Partner in Crime
20	My Musical Debut
23	A Closer Walk
28	Jammin' for God
32	Let Me Tell You 'Bout the Birds and the Bees
34	West Tech
38	Anchor's Aweigh
44	Damn Right
49	A Close Encounter at Sea
51	Change of Command
54	A New Life
59	Walking the Fence
63	Let's Get Serious
67	The Power of Prayer
71	I Want To Hold Your Hand
74	Hit the Road, Jack
77	The Long and Winding Road
92	The Benediction
95	Photo Section

FOREWORD

What a thoroughly enjoyable experience, reading this book!

About the author—- I have known Ed for about nine years. We are in men's group together, and it has become mainly an accountability group. It's a pretty tough group of very strong men, very confrontive, no holds barred. And there is no hiding in this group. So I feel that I know Ed Rothacker very, very well.

Ed has been to the mountaintops, on the fast track of success, making a high income and enjoying everything that comes with it. Also I've seen him in the dark valleys of affliction and adversity (I've come to believe you learn more about a person's character during those times).

Here is what is always apparent: relentless optimism. Ed is always thankful, always in close touch with his Lord, a Lord who somehow seems so far away to so many.

It does not even occur to him to be mainly focused on himself. That alone sets him apart from most people in our culture. And from that great soul flows a deep, warm humanity, and a continuous commitment to what is best for others. And out of that spirit he has gotten this book into your hands.

To me, this book is worthwhile because the writer is worthwhile. And if you read Keys to Glory, you will know my dear friend and brother Ed Rothacker.

Doug Dickson
Metro Director, Columbus, Ohio
CBMC USA

A WEST SIDE STORY

West 116th Street in Cleveland, Ohio, was a fun place to grow up. We're talking 1950s and 60s. Many of the old houses already made the transition to aluminum siding. The front yards were separated by hedges, making practicing for the hurdles in the Olympics a regular event. Our house sat in the middle of the block, a duplex, with my cousins living next door. One end of the street was the public school with a playground including a dirt ball field with a chain link backstop. The other end of the block was the Catholic school—St. Rose of Lima—my school.

I have an older sister, Lenore, named after my mom's mother. I came next, and since my grandfathers were named Edward and Edmund, well? Who eventually followed were Phil, Mark, Margaret, Joe, Rita and Allen. Eight was enough.

My dad was once asked if he was a family man.

"Yes, five boys and three girls," he said.

"Oh, the good Lord smiled on you," answered the man.

Keys to Glory · 11

"Smiled? He laughed out loud!" said my dad.

My mom, Anne, would say that being a devout Catholic, they used the rhythm method for birth control and that's why all eight of their children were musicians.

Large families were more common back then. Heck, just on our street were the Ginnard's, eleven kids, Ropelewski's with eight, Barret's with seven, and Mumaw's with six. You could knock on a couple doors and get a baseball game going. You don't see much, if any, of that today. Nowadays kids have to have a uniform, coach and a willing driver to play sports. We could be playing anywhere in the neighborhood, even down by the railroad tracks, but we always knew when to come home for dinner. At six o'clock every night, the bells in the tower at St. Rose would go off.

My dad, Glenn (like it said on his uniform), worked in the elevator business as a mechanic. Oh, it had its ups and downs, but it paid the bills (his joke, not mine).

He loved to wrestle with us on the floor, pack us up in the station wagon for a ride in the country and get ice cream, or just watch TV with us on the old Muntz black-and-white. I had my own remote control—my brother Joe. With only three channels to choose from it was a pretty easy job. One night the whole family gathered around to see The Beatles on *The Ed Sullivan Show*. None of us could know how historic that event would be, especially my dad.

"See? All you have to do is have long hair and sing 'yeah, yeah, yeah' and make a million bucks!" was his comment.

I was pretty shy as a young kid. I didn't want to go to church because of all the people there. One Saturday afternoon my dad took me over to church, just to walk around it when no one was there. Good thing I got used to it, because by second grade, our whole school through eighth grade had assigned seats every Sunday morning at the 8:30 a.m. Mass with our class. Boys sat on one side of the aisle and girls on the other. It was also in second grade I started piano lessons. My mom played piano and I loved to sit and listen to her. My dad always wanted to learn an instrument, but there wasn't the money for either an instrument or lessons when he was growing up. His desire was to see that every one of his kids had an opportunity to learn a musical instrument.

Before leaving school one day, we were all pinned with a note to take home. Private piano lessons were available at the convent during the school day for $1.50 one half hour each week. It was a no-brainer and my parents signed me up. Sister Agnes Marie was by far the oldest nun in the convent. She was definitely much older than my Grandmas.

She was the only nun who didn't teach a particular grade full time, but instead, taught singing to all the classes. I'd also see her playing the big organ up in the balcony of the church when the boy's choir would sing. She started me off with the basics; time signature, beats, and learning note reading, first the right hand, then the left.

The only time it wasn't fun was when she knew I didn't practice. She would chew me out; up and down and never fail to get out the ruler for my knuckles. During one of these episodes, she caught me glancing down at my new Timex watch I got for my First Communion to see when the session would end. The watch was immediately confiscated and her ranting continued. My parents never really made me practice.

After that day they didn't have to!

FIRST STEP TOWARD GOD

Before making our First Communion, we had to make our First Confession. That was a little scary going into a darkened box and telling the priest, through an orange plastic window, all your sins. My usual confession ended up with a smattering of disobeying my parents, a couple fights with my brothers to maybe a bad word, now and then. You may get a short sermon followed by *the penance*. Penance is usually prayers you say so you would then be absolved of your sins. It could be ten Hail Mary's, five Our Fathers and five Glory Be's. The Glory Be's were short:

> Glory be to the Father and to the Son and to the Holy Spirit, as it was in the beginning, is now and ever shall be, world without end.
>
> Amen.

As time went on, you knew what confessional to avoid. Father Holcomb was about ninety years old and quite

Keys to Glory · 15

hard of hearing. Since there was usually a line on each side of the confessional, and pews just across the aisle, you wanted to confess quietly so as not to alert the world of your misdeeds.

Someone wasn't talking loud enough one afternoon for Father to hear what was being confessed.

"Speak up," said Father in a loud voice.

The lines to that confessional quickly dispersed to the other available confessionals in the church.

Years later I got to serve Mass for Father Holcomb. As an altar boy, your duties were to ring the bells, say the prayers in Latin, serve the priest the water and wine, and assist in communion. One server had the water and another had the wine. They would be poured slowly into the shiny gold chalice the priest was holding. While pouring, when the priest wanted you to stop, he would lift up his hands slightly as a signal. Father Holcomb would take all of the wine, but only a couple drops of water. He'd swish it around then say a couple prayers before drinking it all in one swig.

It's six thirty in the morning, Father, I thought.

A PARTNER IN CRIME

Steve came to the United States from Australia and joined my second grade class at St. Rose in the middle of the school year. His parents were originally from Hungary and the family spoke Hungarian at home.

For years I thought that was how people in Australia spoke.

Steve lived just a block away on the same street. We soon became best friends and would ride bikes together, hop moving trains, fall in love with the same girl at the same time, work paper routes, and go to church. He had a piano at his house, too, and we'd figure out pop songs, including some by The Monkees. We would figure out chords by ear and sing, even if we didn't know all the words. We would dream of being in a band of our own, on stage with screaming girls in the audience.

One day I went over to his house to ride bikes. Steve had gotten in trouble and was grounded. He taught me how to say, *May we go bicycle riding?* in Hungarian. I then repeated the phrase to Steve's mom. She melted, thought it was just precious that I learned a little Hungarian, and promptly let us go.

Just before summer vacation in seventh grade, our class was offered some free courses through the Cleveland Public Schools. Among the courses listed were Spanish, typing and tennis. Steve and I would play tennis but neither of us was good at it. We signed up for tennis. We reported to a high school gym with our rackets and soon found we were the only boys in the class. There were ten girls and us. We had a lot of fun and actually managed to improve our game; including tennis.

In eighth grade we both had the hots for a girl named Liz. At home she was known as Bea. The two eighth grade classes of girls would use our room when the boys were at gym. After one of those room swaps, I left a note in Steve's desk as if it was from Liz for Steve to come over to her house that night. Liz lived a mile or so away, but Steve went, and it rained. He got there, soaking wet, and said he received her note, she replied: "What note?"

He knew right away who did it and the next day after school I was attacked while walking home. We wrestled on the ground in our school clothes—ties and all. We were right across the street from the school and drew quite a crowd. Not because two guys were fighting, but because it was Ed and Steve! It didn't take too long before we were best friends again.

MY MUSICAL DEBUT

During fourth grade Sister Agnes Marie asked if I might help with music when she'd come to our class. She wanted me to play the piano so she could better go up and down the rows listening to the voices.

This was cool! I was the only one in the class who could play piano well enough to accompany the class. Plus I was thrilled to play somewhere besides home and the practice room at the convent.

My music took a giant leap in seventh grade. After I served for morning Mass, put out the candles, hung up the robes, and polished off the wine, the priest pointed to an organ that was placed temporarily behind the curtain just off the altar.

The big Baldwin in the balcony was undergoing some repairs and this one was brought in and hooked up to the sound system.

"Eddy, you play don't you?" he asked.

"Piano, not one of these," I said.

"Why don't you sit down and try it?" he said.

I then peered out from behind the curtain to make sure the church was empty since the only song I knew without music was Alley Cat by Bent Fabric. Here was this huge box with two keyboards, bass pedals and a bunch of switches, lights and knobs. Between the two of us we figured out how to turn it on. I played Alley Cat. It must have sounded like Skateland roller rink on Brookpark Road, but it was good enough for Father.

"You know, I bet with some lessons on this thing, you could play for Sunday Mass," he said.

This was the big time! Wait till I tell Mom and Dad, Steve, everyone! Father had a talk with my piano teacher and lessons were moved from the convent to the church.

After three months of organ lessons, I met with Jack Matthews, the church music director, on a Saturday at the church. We talked near the front of the church for a while.

"Go on up and play a few hymns, then come back down and we'll talk" he said.

I was pretty nervous but I picked some songs I'd been working on, cranked up the volume and let it rip. Afterwards I came back down. He talked about being in charge when

I'm playing. Pick a good tempo and stick with it regardless of what you're hearing from the congregation.

"You're the boss!" he said.

I've been playing in church now for some forty-plus years and that is still the best advice I ever received. He then asked if I could start the following Sunday to play the eight thirty Mass.

Sweet. That's the service the whole school goes to and I'll be the only one not sitting with my class. It's show time! There's a sense of power playing a big church organ with lots of speakers that a piano just can't deliver, especially in a large room with lots of echoes. It was a new and awesome experience for a thirteen year old.

A CLOSER WALK

I've done about every job you could do in a church: altar boy, choirboy, and now organist, and I enjoyed them all. I guess I like being in the presence of God. After all, I believed Jesus was in the tabernacle, the gold box on the altar, where consecrated hosts or wafers were stored. King David in the Old Testament had a heart toward God, people said. I guess I did too.

One job that I hadn't done was to be the priest saying Mass. I was beginning to believe that someday I would. My friend Steve was also sensing the call. We would do his early morning paper route, then attend the six thirty Mass on weekdays, sitting behind the nuns when we could have easily gone back to bed. The only classmates we saw were the ones serving Mass that morning.

There is no comparison to being at peace with God. I felt that warm love and acceptance when I was in church, but didn't know how to take it with me when I left.

My dad had converted the attic into a beautiful dorm

for the boys. It had four sets of twin beds and dressers built end-to-end along the wall. Each dresser had a shelf that could slide out providing a writing surface where we would do our homework. It was a fun place to play and sometimes pray. I would sometimes get my brothers to kneel and pray the rosary with me. Each of the fifty plus beads represented a prayer you would say and would easily take twenty minutes or so to get through.

My favorite rosary was a glow-in-the-dark plastic one. To get it really bright in the dark I'd hang it by the light on the wall. One time it hung too close to the bulb and the face of Jesus melted. I was devastated. Did I do something that was sacrilegious?

"Does praying on a defective rosary still count?" I wondered.

I would pretend I was a priest and say Mass. I'd use some unconsecrated wafers I got from church so we could have Holy Communion. I remember telling my mom that after seminary and ordination the priest would have to buy his own chalice that he'll use at Mass. I asked how we were going to afford one. She kind of brushed me off saying not to worry about that. She didn't want to be deprived of grand kids or figured it was a phase in my life that would pass. Either way, I felt disappointed that she wasn't more supportive of my calling.

I had a chance to witness an ordination. One day the altar boys were invited to attend an ordination. It was held at a beautiful cathedral downtown. At one point in the ceremony the candidates for priesthood laid face down on the floor. What a picture of humility and surrender before a holy God! I loved the Gregorian chant, incense, and ceremony.

I was a lucky guy, being a Catholic born in America, belonging to the one true church. After all, we were taught that Peter was our first Pope. I learned much later Peter had his flaws, but Jesus loved him and used him to spread the gospel anyway.

We were told our job was to spread the Gospels, but what was that? You had to become a Catholic? The Mumaw family, down the street, was the only Protestant family on the block. They had two boys, John, a year older than me, and Randy, who was my age. They belonged to a Methodist church. I wasn't allowed to go there.

One day John asked me why I went to confession. Why couldn't I just talk to God directly, confess my sins, and ask for forgiveness? I didn't have a good answer, but I faked my way through it quoting some doctrinal statement I learned in catechism classes or something. It ended the discussion, for the time being at least, but I was still unhappy with my answer and that bothered me.

Steve and I began our "seeking God" journey in sixth grade by going to church a lot. That was the year one of the girls in our class went home, held up her middle finger, and asked, "Mom, what does this mean?" When asked where she learned that, her reply was, "All the boys in class do it."

Her mom happened to be the president of the Women's Guild at church. She went directly to the monsignor (pastor) of the church, who went to the principal. She then went to Sister Mary Paul, our sixth grade teacher. Sister waited till the girls were away to gym class and proceeded to walk up and down the rows slapping each one of us across the face. No one knew what was up! *Had she gone nuts?*

"Who in this class has *not* used this sign?" she asked, displaying her middle finger.

Steve and I were the only ones who raised our hands and were dismissed with an apology. I can't remember how much time went by, but when we got back together, Dan Ptacek had a fat lip and it was bleeding. Sister figured he was the ringleader. It was a long time before

I even thought of the "F" word. Actually saying it was totally out of the question. I waited till my Navy days since it was everyday language there.

JAMMIN' FOR GOD

The *Home and Flower Show* came to town every spring and there was always something to see and do there. That year, I saw a stage set up with guitars, amps, a portable organ, and microphones. I had never seen a live rock band.

Soon The Pilgrims were introduced and hit the stage playing some songs I heard on the radio. One song was "House of the Rising Sun," by The Animals. It sounded just like the radio version I knew, with organ solo and all. I was mesmerized as I stood looking up at this awesome band. My life dream and goals instantly became clear. I have to get in a band!

I began learning how to play piano by ear. One reason was that Sister Agnes Marie would never teach me to play pop music and the other was I couldn't afford to buy sheet music for everything I wanted to work on. I didn't have a portable organ at home, so I would practice on the church organ when no one was around. I had a key to the church now! I learned "House of the Rising Sun" and it sounded pretty cool in an empty church all cranked up.

The following Sunday my sister Lenore was with me in the balcony for Mass. It was a sold-out crowd, and after singing the four verses of a hymn during Communion, there was still a very long line. The silence was deafening. What was needed was some soothing background music. Got it!

"House of the Rising Sun."

I brought it way down and left out the organ solo so as not to be discovered. It didn't work. A very angry woman met us as we made our way down from the balcony.

"Who was playing the organ?" she demanded to know.

We pointed to each other at first, then I 'fessed up. She read me the Riot Act, saying all she could think about during communion was a house of ill repute. I didn't even know what a house of ill repute *was*.

Once she left, the priest who said the Mass was walking down the center aisle toward us.

"Oh no," I thought. "Here we go."

"What were you playing during communion, Ed?" he asked.

Keys to Glory · 29

"It was 'House of the Rising Sun' by The Animals," I admitted.

"That was pretty, you should play that more often," he said.

I couldn't believe it! I'm off the hook! That just opened the door for lots of possibilities.

There was a small Methodist church across the street from ours. In the basement of the church was a Rec Hall with a bowling alley, ping-pong, and an old upright piano. I was playing around with the piano one day when the big kids suddenly surrounded me. These were the same kids I'd cross the street to avoid—should I encounter them in the neighborhood. They were troublemakers

"Hey Rothacker, do you know how to play The Pink Panther?" one asked in his tough-guy voice.

The first Pink Panther movie was playing at the Granada Theater and the theme song was hitting the airways. I had gotten the sheet music and just started working on it. I positioned both hands on the lower half of the keyboard and played the first four chords:

Da-Dum Da-Dum.

These guys flipped out and thought that was the neatest thing in the world. I was instantly one cool dude and felt my chances of getting beaten up decreased tremendously! It inspired me to work harder at my music, thinking this could really help me get through life.

I was asked to play organ for my Aunt's wedding. I not only played, I sang all the responses from the balcony in Latin. Afterward, I was given a model car for playing. It was my first paid gig! A couple years ago I asked my Aunt how much she remembers about the wedding. She said they walked down the aisle to my processional, got to the front, faced the priest, and waited for the music to stop in order to proceed with the wedding.

The music didn't stop.

She said I kept playing and playing and playing. She asked me why, and I said I worked real hard on that piece and was going to finish it. I must have learned something since then because I now time the whole procession at the rehearsal, so I know when to stop.

LET ME TELL YOU 'BOUT THE BIRDS AND THE BEES

Back then thirteen-year-olds didn't always know the facts of life. Case in point was Roddy Horton, a very bright kid, who always dressed and groomed like his parents had money. In the schoolyard the subject of sex came up and Tom Ropelewski was explaining to Roddy where babies came from.

Roddy refused to believe it, saying his parents would never do such a thing and ended up covering his ears and yelling. Later, Tom was asked by one of the nuns who witnessed some of this from the window what that was all about. Soon after Tom explained what happened, Father Conway was asked to come in and give "The Talk," while the girls were at gym.

Father Neil Conway was fresh out of the seminary, young, handsome, and fun to be around. His family owned a farm and I had been there a couple times swimming in the lake and horseback riding. He would teach religion class and have to field all the "what if" questions we could muster.

"What if a couple was on their way to the church to have their baby baptized when it was killed in an accident? Would the baby go to Heaven or Limbo?" someone would ask.

I guess the church recently rescinded the idea of Limbo. Anyway, I don't know how much experience he had teaching the birds and bees, but he seemed to come through it okay with diagrams on the blackboard and all. To be honest, it answered a few questions for me too. We didn't have MTV back then.

Just a couple weeks later, my dad asked me upstairs and he seemed a little nervous. I saved him some time.

"Father Conway already explained everything to us at school," I said. He asked me a test question to make sure and when I answered correctly, pure relief came over him.

One down, four to go, he thought.

WEST TECH

During my high school years, I continued going to church and playing organ for Mass, though I began to attend a public school. I can't say I was growing spiritually, just going through the motions. I was Catholic and Catholics go to church.

It seemed most of my eighth grade class from St. Rose stopped going, though. It was still my way of staying somewhat close to God. It also looked good on my resume. A girl I started seeing had me over to her house to meet her parents.

"Ed plays the organ at St. Rose's," she said as I was introduced

That seemed to impress them and then they said they were going to the store and would be back in an hour or so. Then they left. My girlfriend was in disbelief and told me they had never before left her home alone with a boy. Just one of the perks for keeping the faith I guess!

My music continued all through high school. Besides

church, I played organ in a rock band with my brother, Phil, as drummer and lead singer; I played piano for choirs at school and would accompany soloists for competitions. There were also roles in a community theater group and in the high school senior play. In the summer of 1969, I was a Jet in *West Side Story*. In the senior play, I was Captain Keller in *The Miracle Worker*.

When our choir teacher took leave for eye surgery, I would lead rehearsals for the ninth grade girl's choir while the substitute teacher stood in the back of the room. That was fun! The only problem happened when walking the hall with my girlfriend; a cute freshman girl walked by and said, "Hi, Eddy," with a sweet little voice

"Who was *that*?" my girlfriend asked, in a stern, not so sweet voice. My response was a calm, "I—I—I don't know."

Being at a technical high school, I was able to major in electricity and electronics. It was four periods a day for both my junior and senior years. My dad took the same courses at East Tech when he was in school. My hope was to follow his footsteps and maybe get into the elevator business too. I loved electronics and was a straight "A" student in it.

"Ed, what activities are you involved in both in and outside of school?" asked Mr. Senser, my electronics teacher.

Keys to Glory · 35

"Well, I'm president of my homeroom, vice president of Key Club, play organ at my church every Sunday, in a community theater group, play in a rock band, on the social committee..."

"Okay, okay," he said as he cut me off. "What I'd like you to do is write an essay on why you chose Vocational Electricity and mention those activities."

He was going to enter my name for a statewide contest sponsored by the Governor's office. A couple months later, while in homeroom, I was called down to the principal's office. I figured they got the wrong Rothacker. It was my brother Phil who always got in trouble. One day while in electronics class, someone came to the door to say Rothacker was wanted at the principal's office.

"No, you want my brother Phil. He's across the hall," I said. I was right.

This time was different. *My* name was on the slip of paper. I was joined outside Mr. Scott's office by another student. Neither of us knew what was going on.

"Boy, you guys really did it this time!" said Mr. Scott when he finally emerged from his office. His stern look turned into a smile and he handed us each a document. We had both won the Governor's Award, signed by the governor himself. Mine was for Vocational Electricity and the other was for Drafting. An announcement went over the school's PA system.

To this day, I kid my brother Phil saying the one time I get called down to the principal's office was to win an award! Phil wasn't a bad kid. He just hung around with the wrong crowd. One day he was brought home by the police. They followed him as he entered the house. My dad was upstairs.

"Hey Dad, the fuzz want to talk to you," yelled Phil.

I can only imagine what my dad was thinking. Someone once said that grandkids are God's gift to parents who didn't kill their kids.

There was a lot of school pride back then. West Tech still had a dress code and there was respect for authority. The hall monitor was a petite lady. She was known as Mousie, but never to her face. You did *not* want to be caught by her in the halls during class without a hall pass. Bussing had not been put in place, so kids could stay after school to be involved in various activities. The purchase of the one bus the school had was made possible by fundraisers organized by the students.

The school was closed in 1995. The building is on the National Register of Historic Places. It is being renovated into luxury apartments. At least it didn't go the way of the wrecking ball.

ANCHOR'S AWEIGH

In 1970, my graduation year, the Vietnam War was still going strong and so was the draft. Rather than wait to see what my draft number would be (picked by lottery), I joined the Navy. I remembered my choir teacher saying something about the Navy's Blue Jacket Choir. I was given an electronics aptitude test which was a breeze. The recruiter guaranteed me a school in electronics after basic training.

I left for boot camp two weeks after graduation. This was my first time out of the state and first time on an airplane. I was headed to Chicago and the Great Lakes Naval Training Center. After getting a buzz haircut and picking up the issued uniforms, we had the opportunity to try out for special units. These included drill team, band, drum and Bugle Corp and, yes, choir. I broke the cardinal rule of the military: Don't volunteer for anything! During my audition I was asked what religion I was.

"Catholic," I said. The choir director pulled out a

Methodist hymnal, turned to a hymn and told me to sing the song by reading the notes without any accompaniment. My reading piano music must have paid off because I made it.

Besides singing for graduations each Friday, and some special events, we also sang in church on Sundays. We were divided into two groups: Catholic and Protestant. Our first rehearsal for church was in the evening with a second-class petty officer as director. It was a nice break from the strict training during the day. Someone was on the organ and struggling to play the music. Then someone else slid on the bench to try and didn't do much better.

"Does anyone here know how to play this thing?" the director finally asked.

I really enjoyed singing but usually got stuck playing the piano just like in high school. Things, however, seemed a little desperate so I slowly raised my hand. I sat on the organ bench, right foot on the volume pedal, both hands on the top keyboard, and played the song all the way through. When I stopped the director was looking at me.

"Now how long were you going to just sit there?" he asked.

I remember playing my portable organ at home the

night before leaving for the Navy and quietly saying goodbye to my music for four years. Now just days after starting my basic training, I'm playing the organ, in the Navy.

There were some nice benefits to being in the choir. One was having practice in the afternoons instead of marching or running the obstacle course in the heat of the summer. Another came when it was announced we were leaving base to sing the National Anthem on Soldier's Field before a Chicago Bears and Minnesota Vikings pre-season football game. And we got to stay for the game. Boot camp was supposed to be hell on Earth. That's what everybody told me.

Oh, it was hard work all right, but I seemed to find a way to make the most of it.

Since second grade, I couldn't remember ever missing Sunday Mass. Having gone through basic training, my track record was still intact. My orders came in. I would be going to Fire Control Technician School (radar for the weapons systems) across the street. There was a beautiful chapel right on the base, the same one we would sing in every Sunday. I continued going.

There was an old upright piano in the Rec Hall so my mom mailed up a bunch of my sheet music. I was still playing!

I decided to go to confession one Saturday. It had been quite a while, so I figured it was time to start fresh again, you know, clean slate. This time, however, I walked out of the church feeling that it wasn't enough. I didn't have the same feeling as a young kid, reconnecting with God. It kind of bugged me, but I didn't know what to do about it.

"For those of you who think a fire control technician *puts out* fires, you're wrong" said our instructor on the first day of school. "We *start* them!"

The fire control radar system locks onto a target then tells the guns or missiles where to point. The computer would factor in things like wind, target and ship's speed and direction. In school, we had to figure all this out on paper. It was all trigonometry.

I went as far as trigonometry III in high school and the other half of the training was electronics. I couldn't believe how well prepared I was for this job that only weeks ago didn't know existed. After this eighteen-week course, I was assigned to the USS Milwaukee, a supply ship, which was currently in the Mediterranean in the middle of a six-month deployment. Now, for sure, my music was over.

However, that was not my first big disappointment.

An all night Saturday flight to Rota, Spain, got me in pretty late. Coupled with jet lag, I woke up at two p.m. on Sunday. I missed church. It was the first time I could remember. I felt horrible. Although there would be a chaplain aboard my assigned ship, he wasn't a Catholic priest. There would be many Sundays I'd be missing church!

In Rota, I met Floyd Shaw. Turned out we were assigned to the same ship and we both went to FT School. He went to one in Bainbridge, Maryland. Floyd was from Memphis and was the first black friend I ever had. We ended up best friends and still stay in touch after all these years. He learned that I played piano when he heard me play the one at the USO in Athens, Greece, where we waited for the Milwaukee to pull in. Once we boarded, I checked the Rec. room. No piano. I guess those things could roll through a wall during rough seas.

It made sense, but still I was disappointed. Quarters was held every day on the flight deck. Each division would gather to receive instructions for that day plus various announcements. It was called the POD for plan of the day.

I was aboard two weeks when one of the announcements was from Ron Richardson, a storekeeper. It read:

Ron Richardson, SK2, is a drummer and looking to put

together a ship's rock band. We could use a couple guitar players. If interested, call ext. 242.

I couldn't believe it! Right after quarters, we were dismissed and I tracked this guy, Ron, down. I told him I have an organ and amp at home and was in a band all through high school. He said, "If you can get that equipment on this ship, you're in the band."

DAMN RIGHT

Now the hard part was getting my equipment aboard. Our homeport in the states was Newport, Rhode Island. When we got back, I flew home to Cleveland and told my dad about the band. I said that I really wanted to be in it. He offered to drive my gear and me back to Newport in the station wagon. It was a little awkward and heavy carrying that stuff up the long gangway to the main deck of the ship, but nothing was going to keep me from this opportunity.

Within a few months we had a six-piece band consisting of guitar, bass, organ, drums, trumpet and sax. We had a ship-wide contest to come up with a name for the band.

One entry, Damn Right, inspired by Isaac Hayes' "Theme from Shaft," was chosen. Floyd learned guitar while on the ship and eventually made it a seven-piece band. We'd play songs by Chicago, Blood, Sweat & Tears, Santana, Three Dog Night, and many others. We not only entertained our own crew from time to time, but also other ships that came alongside for refueling and supplies. Soon we were playing in Officer's Clubs and USOs in Greece, Spain, Italy, and Turkey.

The USO, United Service Organization, serves military personnel by providing morale, welfare and entertainment for men and women in uniform. It was a privilege to participate in their program, but was also a lot of work. In Athens, Greece, for example, our ship was anchored way out in the bay. Our equipment had to be lowered into a boat with cranes before a fifteen minute ride to a pier. We then had to unload everything up onto the pier, and then load onto a truck. We'd then drive downtown to the USO Club which was up a flight of stairs. Our band would play for a couple hours before putting the whole routing in reverse.

One day we had the JFK aircraft carrier coming alongside for fuel and supplies. The captain wanted the band to play for our guests.

"Will the ship's band assemble on the main deck," came over the speaker system.

This was always a fun time for everyone. The crew enjoyed listening to us, and we loved to play. We also got out a lot of work.

We set up our amps, microphones and instruments, and then powered everything on. We began getting a very loud intermittent hum coming out of our amplifiers. It was so loud; I thought we were going to blow the speakers out. It was coming from a huge rotating radar dish on the carrier. We had to shut everything down. We used a headset to communicate to the bridge to explain why we couldn't play.

"Wait one," was their response.

"Wait one?" we said to ourselves. "Wait for what?"

Within a couple of minutes, that radar came to a screeching halt.

"Try it now," was the word from the bridge. Everything worked fine.

There was some big NATO conference, which brought about thirty ships to Izmir, Turkey. Since many of the ships had bands, someone took the opportunity to put together a battle of the bands. We were one of about seven bands competing that night.

Our opener was "Dance to the Music" by Sly and the Family Stone. The place went nuts.

We were a hit. After playing our twenty minutes or so, the crowd did not want us to leave and make room the other acts. The organizer asked if we could play again once the other bands finished. That announcement settled down the audience, and we came back to play three more hours of music. We won the title, "Best Band in the Sixth Fleet."

Word got to the band that the Admiral was in attendance that night. He wanted our band to travel to Munich, Germany to play for some Officers Clubs there. The Olympics were also going on in that city. We were excited about that news and couldn't wait to go.

Unfortunately, about two weeks later, our ship was ordered to assist in efforts off the coast of Vietnam. Things were really heating up there. That order superseded the Admirals wishes so Munich was out. It was October of 1972.

Our journey to the Far East took us down and around the African coast. The Suez Canal was not an option for us at the time. I crossed the equator for the first time.

While halfway around Africa, a message came in saying that our band was chosen to represent the entire 6th Fleet in the All Navy Talent Contest to be held in San Diego. The morning after we arrived in the Philippines, we were flown back to the states with layovers in Okinawa, Tokyo, and Honolulu (your tax dollars hard at work!). We were one of seventeen acts representing the

Navy worldwide. We came in second place and I got to go home for a few days spending Thanksgiving and my twenty-first birthday with my family.

A CLOSE ENCOUNTER AT SEA

On a supply ship it was common to have many jobs. I could be working on one of our two fire control radar systems, driving a fork lift truck, directing helicopters landing on our flight deck, or shooting over the first line to a ship we were about to refuel. We also had to stand four-hour watch around the clock while at sea. One watch that our division was responsible for was the fantail watch.

This was an area at the far rear (*aft*, for you sailor types) of the ship just under the helicopter deck. At night, it was so dark you couldn't see your hand in front of your face. Hopefully, you'd hear someone yelling if they fell overboard. You would be their only hope for survival as we had instant communication with the bridge. The hardest watch back there was the mid-watch, which went from midnight to 0400. It was boring and sometimes difficult to stay awake.

One of my mid-watch's was on a clear night with no

moon. I never saw so many stars in my life. I lost count of the number of shooting stars there were. There's nothing like a view of the sky from the middle of the ocean! It inspired me to pray. I began thanking God for his creation, my family, my girlfriend back home, the friends I made on the ship, the band, and countries I had a chance to visit. I was projecting those prayers light years away, beyond the stars, where God was. Before I knew it, a tap on the shoulder told me I was being relieved and could go to bed for a couple hours. I wasn't finished praying. It was the fastest four hours I ever experienced. There was no priest, no choir, no music, no communion, but I had just been in church.

CHANGE OF COMMAND

During a North Atlantic cruise, we had a chance to be part of a rescue operation.

"Emergency flight quarters, emergency flight quarters" rang over the speaker system throughout the ship. Since flight ops was one of my duties, I was relieved from my usual underway watch and ran up several sets of stairs to the flight deck. We had the cargo nets lowered, the area cleared, the crash team ready with foam, wearing their asbestos suits. About a mile away was an anti-submarine warfare helicopter, one of ours, with major mechanical problems looking for a place to set down. We were the closest ship. As we watched it getting closer and closer, the tail rotor suddenly flew off and the craft began spinning and going down fast. We were totally helpless. There was nothing we could do. We all just stood there in shocked silence. Only two of the three crewmen were rescued. The one who didn't make it had a wife and kids back home. Within an hour it was learned that during this crisis, the ship's chaplain was on the bridge, not saying a prayer for these three guys' safety, but rapidly taking photos with his telephoto, auto-advance, 35mm camera. I guess my shipmates lost all respect for him and it wasn't long after his transfer was arranged. I don't know if he was fairly judged. That was the last chaplain I saw on that ship.

Jim Natter was an ensign fresh from the Naval Academy. He looked so young and was eager to get at his new assignment. He was always with a smile on his face, very positive and upbeat. He would leave pamphlets around that talked about God and being saved.

He single-handedly got all nude pinups taken down from lockers and the workspaces. People didn't know what to make of this guy. It was hard not to like him, but he was different. It was announced at quarters one morning that Ensign Natter would be holding ecumenical church services in the band room (our space) on Sunday mornings. I found out ecumenical meant, "y'all come." I went. I ended up playing organ as we learned some new songs. We had about ten guys show up. Mr. Natter read some passages out of the Bible, provided a little exposition, prayed a little, we sang a little, and then we were done. The Bible says, "For where two or more are gathered together in my name, there am I in the midst of them" (Matthew 18:20 NAB).

God *was* there. Our little services and times together were a welcomed oasis for my spirit.

A NEW LIFE

In June of 1974 my four-year hitch was up and I went back to Cleveland and promptly got back on staff of St. Rose of Lima church as one of their organists. It felt good to be back!

After a short stint working second shift at a factory, I auditioned for a band. Alan Broze was singer, front man, and entertainer who was in the process of putting together a new backup band. The audition took place at my house where I had a Hammond organ and electric piano set up. I played along with a tape of a couple Top Forty songs by The Doobie Brothers, Edgar Winter, and Bachman Turner Overdrive.

I made the band and soon we were playing some pretty nice rooms, like The Brown Derby and some hotels. We usually played the same place for a week or two, which allowed us to leave most of our equipment setup. One of these clubs was a place on the far eastern side of Cleveland called the Shangri La. Every Friday night was free taco night.

Alan's wife, Connie, worked as a waitress in Lakewood and one night showed up with a friend from work who was also a waitress.

I was introduced to Pat. Connie pulled me aside and suggested we all go to breakfast after the gig. I was already pretty tired, and the drive back to the Westside was about forty minutes. I suggested she ask Mike, our guitar player; maybe he'd be interested.

During one of our sets, I noticed some guy sitting next to Pat at the bar. He appeared to be hitting on her. Why this bothered me, I'm not sure. I just had to break this up.

As soon as we took our next break, I made a beeline to Pat and began talking with her like we were old friends so this guy would take a hike. I liked her and asked if she wanted to go to breakfast with Alan and Connie. Pat was a single mom. Jeffery was nine years old and a neat little kid.

We went to her house after breakfast to listen to some music when the conversation turned to God. She talked about Jesus like someone she knew personally. She said she had been saved and would be in heaven when she died. How can this be? For all the years I attended church, altar boy, choirboy, organist, and all around pretty good guy, I did not have that same assurance.

"I always believed if your goods outweighed your bads when you died, you'd make it to heaven," I said.

"If we could earn our way into heaven, then why did Jesus have to come?" Pat asked. She went on to explain that Jesus' death on the cross was payment for my sins. I needed to ask for forgiveness, accept Jesus as my Savior and Lord and begin a new life living for him.

It almost sounded too simple. The last words Jesus spoke on the cross were, "It is finished," after all. What were finished were animal sacrifices in the temple and trying to please God in our own power. The Holy Spirit was given to the apostles on Pentecost to give them the power to live for God and boldly preach salvation to the world. That's the gospel! I knew I wanted what Pat had.

A couple weeks later we were at the home of Pat's cousin Michelle. She is the one who prayed with Pat just a month ago to receive Christ. She asked if I wanted to pray with her to receive Christ and I said I did. I knelt in front of their couch in the living room and we prayed. There were no stained glass windows, no incense, or music, but I was saved that night! I knew that something had taken place in my life immediately. I never felt this way walking out of the confessional. There is a joy that comes from being born into God's kingdom; that's why we were created in the first place, to be in his presence and worship him. That was the position Adam and Eve were in, but they wanted more. There *was* nothing more. They chose to disobey God and were separated by sin. When they realized what they did, they covered themselves with fig leaves. They invented religion. I call it the religion of fig leaves. It was man's first attempt to get back in the graces of a holy God by covering it up. It was the work of man. It was their way, not God's way. We are told in scripture that, "… without the shedding of blood, there is no forgiveness" (Hebrews 9:22 NAB).

God himself initiated the first shedding of blood to cover sin. In Genesis, we're told that God clothed Adam and Eve in animal skins. Animal blood was shed. It was a foretelling of Christ, who would eventually shed his own blood for the sins of the whole world. He was the Lamb of God. The fig leaves didn't cut it and neither does anything we do apart from God's will.

The religions of the world basically teach the way to gain favor with God is through our own goodness or works. We are powerless to bridge that gap on our own.

True Christianity is the only one where God initiates forgiveness and intimacy.

"For God so loved the world that He gave His only Son, so that everyone who believes in him, might not perish but might have eternal life," (John 3:16 NAB).

Another translations says, "…whoever believes in him" (NIV).

A couple key words in these verses are "gave" and "whoever." If I was *given* a gift, I wouldn't feel obligated to pay for it; otherwise, it wouldn't be a gift. It was given out of love, but I can choose not to receive it. In the spring of 1975, I became a "whoever." I chose to receive it.

WALKING THE FENCE

I had an insatiable appetite for the Word of God. We only had one Bible at home and it weighed about fifteen pounds. It was used to record births, marriages, deaths, and other events. As a youngster, I remember flipping through it looking at the colored illustrations. It was not read at home and can't say it was really encouraged by my school or church. I thought it was too difficult to understand and needed help interpreting it.

Now I'm traveling with a lounge band. It was called Alan Broze and Parade. Our theme song was "Don't Rain on My Parade" from Funny Girl. We would vamp to that song as an opening and before each break. Alan was a very talented front man, always winning over the crowd. His style was a cross between Bobby Vinton and Wayne Newton. We played a wide range of music to satisfy almost any venue.

We could go from Frank Sinatra to Bad Company then a Broadway medley. We'd usually play four to five sets a night each running about forty-five minutes long. When the band first formed, we didn't have a bass player. I had a separate little keyboard allowing me to play bass with my left hand. This was similar to the way Ray Manzarek of The Doors played. The furthest we traveled between gigs was from Canton, Ohio, to Key West, Florida. We were actually late for that one. We were supposed to open on a Monday night but didn't arrive till then. We still needed to set up and shower before we could play.

"Mondays are generally slow anyway" said the owner. "Why don't you guys set up your gear then hit the swimming pool."

That sounded fabulous, especially since my 1972 Ford Econoline van was not equipped with air conditioning. When playing at hotels, the rooms were included. We didn't have to share rooms as we each had our own. Not so when rooms were not included. When it came out of our pocket, we'd choose the cheapest place we could find and would double up.

I picked up my first Bible from a hotel room where our band was playing. The Gideon's placed it. We ended up doing quite a bit of traveling and I soon found the lifestyle of a road musician conflicted with what happened inside of me. I was uncomfortable in certain situations that used to be okay. It wasn't like I have to behave in a certain way now that I'm a professing follower of Christ. My desires actually were beginning to change. Off-color humor was not funny to me anymore. I was beginning to feel out of place.

Wherever we were, I would look for a Bible-teaching church on Sunday. In Tallahassee, Florida, I called a Christian bookstore for advice on a good church. I was sent to a high school where a couple hundred, mostly young people, were worshipping and praising God to upbeat contemporary music. There was a lot of hugging. I brought Dan, my bass player, with me. The whole group prayed for the both of us. This was family! I just met these folks, but we were instantly accepted. It was an awesome experience.

Some months later, we were playing in Fort Lauderdale at a nice Best Western, and were offered a permanent job as house band. We all got apartments and settled in. After three months, I felt a little burned out. Same place, same songs, same groupies, but new temptations. Drug use in the band was a daily event.

One night, a couple of the guys were trying out some cocaine they bought from a dealer across the street. I was offered some, which would have been a new experience for me, but I said no thanks. I soon made plans to quit the band and head back to Cleveland.

I joined my brother's band thinking that would be a much better environment but it wasn't. It wasn't the other guys; it was me, in the same lifestyle. When we got back to Cleveland after about a three-month tour, I was let go. My brother said they couldn't afford a keyboard player and needed to go back to being a trio. I had a fleeting thought of looking for another band.

That thought lasted less than a minute before hearing a word from God: "Enough!"

"You're right. I know," I said. Hearing from God was relatively new for me, but this was unmistakable.

LET'S GET SERIOUS

I had not used any of my veteran's benefits for schooling and I'd always wanted to give college a shot, so I enrolled in a community college with my major in music. Pat had begun attending a Foursquare Gospel Church a number of months previously. I had visited it once with her while on a quick home visit. I remember the pastor, Bob Hils, a big guy whose laugh and smile were infectious. Bob said they would pray that I wouldn't have to play in bars for a living and could come play organ for them. There was a big Hammond console that was not being used.

"Yeah, that would be great!" I said, but deep down I was saying, "Fat chance, pal!"

I guess I was enjoying the road too much then, while they had begun to earnestly ask God for an organist. When I came back, it was to stay. Church was Sunday morning, Sunday night and Wednesday night. Bob was an awesome teacher and Bible scholar and I was like a sponge taking it all in.

Shortly after I began attending, I was told of a couple guys at the church, Tom and Andy, who both played guitar and have a band, that I should go and hear play. I thought, *How cute, a little band*. Of course, I was "Mister Cool" professional, just coming off the road.

Heck, we made a 45 rpm and were on TV once. Who were these Tom and Andy guys? I went one night to a coffee house called The Living Room where they were playing. They played mostly original music on acoustic guitars, very melodious, with beautiful harmonies, giving praise to God. I kept hearing piano parts in my head as I was listening.

"How could I possibly ask to be a part of this ministry with the attitude I had before walking in?" I thought. I was humbled. When they were done for the night, Tom asked if would be interested in bringing my piano to the next rehearsal.

"Sure!" I answered, with excitement. The band known as Tom and Andy, became *Yesterday, Today and Forever* from the Book of Hebrews, which says: "Jesus Christ is the same, yesterday, today and forever" (Heb 13:8 NAB).

When I finished my first year at college, I began working for a guy from our church named Bill Hodge.

He was about my dad's age, but sure didn't act like it. He loved life, people, hard work and good food. You'd never see Bill at a fast food restaurant. He had a couple businesses: kitchen and bath remodeling, and was owner of the Good Reading Company.

He put spinner-racks of inspirational paperbacks in drug stores and convenient stores. Anywhere he could find room and a willing customer. A large drug store chain gave him the okay to go in over thirty of their stores in northeast Ohio. A part-time ministry was turning into a full time job. I had a van and would make deliveries, do billing, and research new titles. I loved it. I was out and about, could plan my own day, and was in a very good position to share my faith.

When I was done with my rounds, about ninety locations, I'd meet Bill on the job. I learned quite a bit about home improvement and also about being a bold witness. Bill would talk about Jesus with whomever, wherever. He was in a small restaurant near our office one day, while three guys were talking at the counter.

"You'll never guess who I saw the other day ... George Henderson," one man said.

"Jesus Christ! I haven't seen George in years!" another exclaimed loudly.

"Hey I know him!" chimed Bill.

"You know George Henderson?" asked one of the men.

"No, I know Jesus Christ!" Bill said. All three of them just looked with dropped jaws. It was sweet. He had a way of letting people know where he stood without being "holier than thou." It can be done.

Bill led a monthly church service at a juvenile detention home on the near east side. A few of us would join him to provide some music and support. These kids were hurting, and receptive to the gospel. We would use an analogy of a kid in front of a judge, waiting to be sentenced for car theft. Just then, someone steps forward and asks to be sent to jail instead of the thief. He was put away while the kid went free.

When asked what their response would be to an offer like that, the place would erupt with joy.

"That's exactly what Jesus did for you," Bill said.

Many would come forward to pray to receive Christ and we would distribute Bibles to the whole group. Often they would request prayer for a younger sibling so they wouldn't make the same mistakes in life. It was always a powerful time.

THE POWER OF PRAYER

My next-door neighbor, Eleanor, was a Christian with a prayer ministry. She and her friend Katie had been praying for me since high school.

"Eddy is going in the Navy, and you know what *that* means," Eleanor would tell Katie, and they continued to pray.

"Eddy's in a band now and you know what *that* means," she said, and they kept praying. I didn't find all this out till years later. Sometimes God will lay something on my heart to pray about or a name pops in my head from seemingly nowhere. It's usually time to pray. We might not even see the results of those prayers in this life, but sometimes we do.

I joined a small-group Bible study with some folks from my church and we met in one of their homes. I didn't know everybody. We were asked to go around the room, introduce ourselves and tell how we came to know the Lord.

Keys to Glory · 67

As I was sharing my story, one lady was looking at me with a funny look on her face. She asked where I lived. I told her West 117th Street, between Detroit and Franklin avenues.

She asked if I knew Eleanor.

"Yeah, she lives next door," I said.

"You're Eddy!" She blurted out, nearly crying. It was Katie. She'd never known me but had been praying for me for about seven years. God put us in the same church and now in the same room with a small Bible study group.

I wasn't dating during this time and I really missed it. It was beginning to get to me and I remember praying one day to God that I felt lonely. Oh, I had lots of friends, but at church I seemed to be the most eligible bachelor around. After service, we usually played the closing song again, as people would leave or mingle. As I was cranking that old Hammond, a number of young school-age girls would come up and hang around till I was done playing. It was nice having fans, but they were way too young. I talked with Katie one day about it.

"Do you believe God has someone picked out for you?" She asked one day.

"Yes, I can believe that," I said.

"Have you ever prayed for her?" she asked.

"No," I said, "I don't know who she is."

"But God does! Maybe she's not a Christian, yet, and God wants to make her whole before putting you two together. Maybe she has a tough decision to make. In faith, begin praying for her."

I did. It felt a little strange at first, but I prayed for whoever she was.

Weeks later the wife of our assistant pastor, Heidi, came up to me before the morning service started and introduced me to Cindy. She had known Cindy since they were in grade school. I was polite.

"Welcome to our church and hope you enjoy the service," I said. Beverly, our pastor's wife (yes, that would make her Beverly Hils), opened up the service by asking who had a tough week. A number of people raised their hands, including Cindy (I had a good view of everyone from where I sat). I thought it was neat that Cindy felt comfortable enough to participate like that and when she looked my way, I gave her a wink.

I came up to her after the service and asked why she had a tough week. She said she had just broken up with a guy she'd been dating for four years, when Heidi invited her to church.

"Thank you Lord, I'll take it from here!" I said, in my

mind. Some guys need a two by four across the head to figure things out. Mine came that morning. What were the chances of a good-looking woman, and available, even coming to our small church in inner city Cleveland anyway? With God, all things are possible!"

I WANT TO HOLD YOUR HAND

We began seeing each other on a fairly regular basis. I told her that my route the next day was going to take me to the drug store just across the street from her apartment. When I got there I found a note sticking out of one of the books. It was a note from Cindy wishing me to have a nice day. I remember telling her once that before we met, I prayed for her. We found out that was the exact time she had decided to break up with her boyfriend. He was not a Christian; in fact, he was raised in an atheist home. She felt he wanted to believe, but his relationship to God was through her. It doesn't work that way. She felt strongly to break it up, even though many of her friends were married and had started families. She'd be starting over, but she felt it was what God wanted.

One of our first dates together was attending a charismatic Catholic service by invitation of my brother Mark. It was a bit livelier than Mass as I remembered. During the Mass, we were asked to share a prayer request with someone next to us and pray. Cindy had told me earlier that her dad was going in for tests on his heart the next day. He'd already had bypass surgery a few years prior. I turned and took Cindy's hands in mine.

"Let's pray for your dad," I said. I asked God to be with the doctors and to heal her dad.

No one had ever done that with her before, let alone a guy she was dating. That little act was such a comfort to her. Deep down all women want a man to be the spiritual head of the house. It is God's plan for the family. In Ephesians, we read: "For the husband is head of his wife just as Christ is head of the church, he himself the savior of the body" (Eph 5:23 NAB).

Verse twenty-five says, "Husbands love your wives, even as Christ loved the church and handed himself over to her…" (Eph 5:25 NAB).

Guys, don't leave it to your wife to be the spiritual head of the home. If you're sitting home while your wife takes the kids to church, you are not in God's will.

Two weeks after we met, I proposed. She said yes, but was concerned her parents might think she was on the rebound and jumped into this too soon.

It was time to meet the parents. To top it off, at the time my hair was a little long and I was sporting a full beard.

We met them at their house and I noticed a baby grand piano in the front room. Cindy told her dad I played and he immediately got out his trumpet, threw some music in front of me, and we had an instant jam session.

We ended the set with the song "The Way We Were," which came out sounding like we'd rehearsed it for weeks.

"I'm in!" I remember thinking. Her dad asked what plans I had for my music. I wasn't sure why he was asking that. Was this a trick question? I told him I had no more plans trying to make a living with it and I would play for church, my Christian band, and just for fun.

"Good answer," he said.

I learned later he used to play trumpet professionally and traveled a lot, which was responsible for the break up of his first marriage.

HIT THE ROAD, JACK

Even though I had already proposed, Cindy's parents did not know. I wanted to make our engagement official by Christmas, just a couple months away, but it was important for me to get her dad's approval.

Dave Balliett was very active in the Methodist church, and had an older brother who was a pastor. He was one of the most generous and caring people I'd ever met. He owned Ball Chemical Company, which provided janitorial supplies to businesses, schools, and churches. It was a very successful business.

One night I was helping him put a pantry door back on its track in their kitchen.

"I want to marry Cindy," I said after a few minutes.

"You don't say?" he said after a long pause that seemed like eternity. We finished the door and joined Cindy and her mom in the family room. He then turned to his wife, Olga.

"Ed wants to marry our daughter."

Cindy looked surprised because she didn't think I was going to do it. Now the interrogation started. I was asked about my finances, career goals, and other resources. I was self-employed at the time with next to nothing saved up. That didn't go over too well. He couldn't see how we would make it and was opposed to the idea of us getting married.

Deep down, I knew God brought us together. I needed to get my two-cents into this conversation. It was my turn.

"I know what you're saying. But if I had $50,000 in the bank, it wouldn't take a whole lot of faith to start a family. The Bible is full of promises where God said he would provide for our needs. It says how he takes care of the birds in the air, how much more will he provide for us."

I shared how I'd given my heart and life to Christ two years ago and how much I've grown spiritually.

"I'm trusting that God will be there for us."

Inside I was trembling. I didn't want to sound preachy, but I had to say what I felt and believed.

"You have my blessing, let's pray about it," he said, after an eternal silence.

The four of us stood up and held hands in a little

circle while my future father-in-law prayed and asked God to bless our decision and our lives together.

Soon Cindy and I left in her car.

"Wow, that was unbelievable wasn't it?" she said.

"Uh, well, uh," I stammered. I was still shaking inside and couldn't even talk. I felt totally drained, too, as I had never done anything like that before in my life. Obviously it was the right thing to do and God blessed it. The wedding was in August, ten months after we had met.

THE LONG AND WINDING ROAD

God *was* there for us. Two kids and a couple jobs later I was offered a sales position and would open a new office in Detroit selling data communications equipment. I was making good money so Cindy wouldn't have to teach and we were buying a nice brick ranch home in a suburb of Detroit. The day we flew up to close on the house was the day my father-in-law died.

It was like God waited to take him until he saw how our faith and steadfastness would be rewarded. I miss him.

We moved in to our new home outside of Detroit on a cold December day. Nathan, who was two years old, was running up and down the ramp of the moving van.

By the end of the day, the beds were set up and furniture was in place. Stories were read to the kids and we finished with nightly prayers. Cindy and I crashed in the family room exhausted. I could tell she was feeling stressed out and depressed. Her dad had just passed away and we moved one hundred eighty miles from her mom and our home. She had to learn her way around, make new friends and find a church. Guys seem to adjust to new surroundings easier. Once I had the stereo set up, it was home.

The doorbell rang. We looked at each other with puzzled expressions on are faces.

"Who could that be?" I wondered.

Our new next-door neighbor, Char, stood there with a pot of decaf and some cookies.

"Are you guy's normal people?" she inquired. She was sent by God!

I love her already, I thought. The previous owners had gone through a bitter divorce. I eventually found a stash of empty whiskey bottles behind the paneling in the garage. No wonder she asked if we were normal. Cindy lit up as we welcomed her into our messy house that was still strewn with boxes. Char was also a Christian and invited us to church. She spent a lot of time with Cindy telling her how to get around town and where the nearest grocery store was.

After Char left, Cindy was almost giddy. She remembered a couple weeks before the move, someone in our home bible study had prayed for her.

"Lord, I pray for Ed and Cindy for a smooth transition to their new home," she prayed. "And I ask Lord that you lead them to a good bible-teaching church and Christian fellowship." She paused, "In fact Lord, I pray that the very day they move in, Cindy meet a Christian woman."

Some people can get carried away with their prayers. Cindy thought this was one of those times. However, God answered that specific prayer. God was even in Michigan!

I was the only person in the Detroit office; but not for long. I saw early on the potential for sales in that market was more than I could handle alone. Soon one of my customers, Kurt Loock joined the sales force. Janet was then hired as secretary. Both Kurt and Janet were Christians. Bob Manzitti was hired as the third salesman. Bob had been in the business for sometime and had a lot of contacts. He was a nice guy too, just not a Christian. He was quick with off-color jokes, even in mixed company. He didn't judge us for our beliefs, nor did we judge him. We just prayed for him.

One Sunday morning at around seven, the phone rang. It was Bob. He told me he and his wife Jane were expecting their first child. When they first found out, they were a little scared as they hadn't planned on starting a family so soon. As the weeks went on, they began getting excited about the idea and were looking forward to it. Jane had been experiencing some bleeding. They were afraid she was going to have a miscarriage. Bob was calling for prayer.

"Ed, I know you have a hot-line," said Bob.

I'm usually not God's man of faith that early in the morning.

"Bob, God is going to show you who He is through this," I said. "We take prayer request before God as a congregation every Sunday, and we'll pray for you guys and that little one this morning"

It just came out. When I hung up, I hoped I didn't just put God on the spot. But the more I thought about it; those words were from God Himself. I was just the messenger.

Within a day, the bleeding stopped and some months later, Eric, with a full head of beautiful red hair was born.

A couple years later, Bob came down with meningitis. He was very sick. Kurt and I went to the University of Michigan Hospital to see him. I knew I had to pray with him while we were there. The laying on of hands may not be something Kurt was accustomed to from his background, but he's going to get a crash course.

Bob was not able to even raise his head up because of the intense pain. This was serious stuff. In his room, there was a burn victim who also had visitors.

"Bob, can we pray with you?" I asked as we were getting ready to leave.

"Sure!" he said. I led, praying out loud, not caring who else was listening.

Within days, he went home. The doctors had no explanation for Bob's speedy recovery.

A few more years passed. The phone rings and its two in the morning. It's Bob. He is sobbing like a little kid. I knew his mother was recovering from heart surgery, but this time it was his dad.

He had a major artery that lead to his heart burst. Bob was calling from the hospital where his dad was in intensive care. He sounded so helpless as he waited for his brother and sister to arrive. By now Cindy was awake.

"Who is it? she asked.

"It's Bob," I answered. "We need to pray for him and his dad."

We prayed with him over the phone, and then hung up. I could not go back to sleep.

"I have to go," I said to Cindy. I got dressed and drove to the east side of town where I was the least familiar.

"Dear God, I pray for Bob's dad," I prayed while driving. "Please send an angel to comfort Bob and his family."

"I'm sending you," said a voice that rang in my head. It may just well have been audible. It was *that* clear!

I had my arm around Bob when the doctor came out to the waiting room.

"I'm sorry. We did all we could," said the doctor. "Would you like to see him?"

As Bob followed the doctor into the operating room, he motioned for me to come too.

I watched as Bob put his head on his father's chest and cried.

"Dad, Dad," he said as if trying to bring him back.

"Bob, he's no longer there," was all I could say. We hugged. I met the rest of the family and had prayer with them all before returning home. I was not emotionally prepared for that night, but hoped somehow God used me.

Bob had never spoken about these events. He referred to himself as the tough, fat Italian.

It's now 1995 and I'm leaving the Detroit office to go to the Columbus branch. It was not a transfer; in fact the company didn't want me to make the move. My wife and I decided we wanted to move back to Ohio and closer to family. Glenn Vraniak was the branch manager then who suggested a "going away" lunch. There were about ten people in the office by then including three technicians. At the restaurant, Glenn suggested everyone take turns telling an "Ed story." After twelve years, there were a lot of stories. We had a lot of fun together. It was a great group of friends I was leaving. They went around the table until it was Bob's turn.

"I will never forget when Ed came to the hospital and was with me when my father died," said Bob. He was usually the first one with the joke or wisecrack. Most at that table had never seen that side of Bob. He was truly grateful and dead serious. I took it as thanks to God, answered prayer and to friendship.

A few years later, Bob gave his heart and life to Jesus Christ making Him his Savior and Lord. He began attending Bible studies and is serving God today.

Now, our two kids are grown. Nate plays drums and lives in Los Angeles (you know what *that* means). Julie is married with 3 kids and is a part-time massage therapist. Her husband Gabriel is a computer network technician.

The Lord has always been in the center of our family, has blessed us abundantly and gotten us through a lot of rough times. My wife and I lead worship for our Sunday school kids at church. I'm at the piano while

Cindy leads the singing and teaches hand motions that go with the songs. I keep up my rock-and-roll by playing occasionally with a couple bands. I have had many opportunities to lead people to Christ. Many of these folks are formerly Catholic who either stopped going to church or were not growing in their faith.

I've been more open about my faith the last few years. After recovering from quadruple heart bypass surgery in 2004, the important things in life matter to me so much more than material things. There are also very practical applications to one's faith like dealing with today's pressures and stress.

"If you had all the worry in the world plus fifteen cents, you could get a cup of coffee," my dad told me when I was young.

The problem was, my dad could never stop worrying about all of us kids. Even after being retired for many years, he had a tendency to spend too much time worrying. Earlier this year, I visited my dad and shared something I learned to do.

"Dad, just a few days ago, I was having a hard time falling asleep," I said. "I was busy thinking about our finances, my job, our son living so far away from home and whatever else was bothering me. With my eyes still closed, I pictured a small box about the size of a cigar box. I opened it up and began putting all these problems into that box, one by one. I closed it up and slid it onto our bookcase headboard of our bed. I said, "'God, these are yours. Please take care of them. I need to get some sleep.' In less than two minutes I was fast asleep."

"Where can I get one of those boxes?" asked my dad.

Father's Day was coming up. I decided to get my dad a box. Cindy found a nice one at a craft store. It was dark brown and looked like a leather chest with a small latch. I took it to a trophy store that does engraving.

"Hi" I said to the lady behind the counter as I walked in. "Can you help me out with a Father's Day gift?"

"What do you need?" she asked.

I showed her the box then told her about my vision and talk with my dad. I asked if they could engrave a scripture verse that would somehow adhere to the top of the box. The verse I chose says, "Cast all your worries upon him because he cares for you" (1 Peter 5:7 NAS).

She assured me that it could be done. We decided on a font and style and it would be ready on Tuesday.

When I returned to the store to get the box, I was told it wasn't ready yet.

"Our computer was down all morning and we just

got it working an hour ago" said the same lady I met days before. "It should be ready in about two hours"

"I'm going to see my daughter in Springfield then so I'll come by tomorrow" I said heading toward the door.

"I've been reading that scripture verse over and over lately," she said.

"Really"? I said.

"My son has been in and out of rehab centers for both alcohol and drug abuse. He's in the hospital now where they discovered his blood sugar levels are over 500," she said with some fear and pain in her face.

"What's your son's name?" I asked.

"Brian," she said.

We were the only ones in the store at the time.

"Could we pray for Brian right now?" I asked.

She nodded and we both bowed our heads as I prayed out loud. Included in my prayer was asking God to heal Brian emotionally, physically and spiritually.

"Thank you," she said as she reached out to grab my hand.

As I got into my car, I felt a wave of emotions over what just took place. I also thanked God for using me to help minister somehow to this woman. She didn't know me from Adam. But she felt comfortable enough to pour out her heart. What a blessing!

The following day I came back. This time there were two ladies behind the counter. The one I had met was with a customer. The younger one went in the back room and came out with my box. They did a beautiful job. The lettering was a bright gold color on a black plate. I reached into my pocket for my wallet.

"No charge," she said.

"What do you mean?" I said digging for some bills.

"My mom insists," was her final offer.

"Did she tell you the story behind the box?" I asked.

"Yes. She also told me that you prayed for my brother," she said gratefully.

When we plant little mustard seeds in the name of Jesus Christ, we can just stand back and watch them grow!

The following Saturday my wife and I went to Cleveland to see my dad. I asked if he remembered our discussion about my imaginary box. He did.

"Well, I got one for you. It's slightly used," as I shared my time at the trophy store. My instructions were for him to write down a prayer request on a piece of paper. Pray about it; then put the paper in the box and close the lid as a symbol of giving it over to God.

I learned a lot about God during my Catholic school years. I learned about a holy God who not only created the universe, but who made me in his image and likeness. I had a fear and awe of God, but I felt he'd punish me at the drop of a hat if I screwed up. It wasn't until years later I learned how the Holy Spirit would live in me and gently guide me in the ways of the Lord. I made the transition from guilt to grace. I didn't have to go to a building to be near God. In fact, the Bible says: "The God who made the world and everything in it, the Lord of heaven and earth, does not dwell in sanctuaries made by human hands...." (Acts 17:24 NAB).

And in 1 Corinthians we read: "Do you not know that your body is a temple of the holy spirit within you, whom you have from God....?" (1 Cor 6:19 NAB).

In the Old Testament, the high priest was the only person who could enter the "Holy of Holies," or the inner sanctum of the temple where God resided. He would offer animal sacrifices and sprinkle blood on the altar for the sins of the people. A curtain or veil separated the priest from the people. "Tell the Israelites to procure for you a red heifer that is free from every blemish and defect" (Numbers 19:2 NAB).

God doesn't want leftovers; he wants our best. He

gave us his best, his only Son, also without blemish or defect. During Jesus' trial in Jerusalem, Pilot said, "I find no guilt in him" (John 19:6 NAB).

One translation says: "I find no fault in him" (John 19:6 KJV).

He was an acceptable sacrifice in the eyes of the Father. There were some major differences to the sacrifices of the past. This was God's own son, and he didn't remain in the tomb, but he rose again because death had no hold on him.

Also, this was the final sacrifice; the last time blood would be shed for the forgiveness of sin. "For Christ also suffered for sins once, the righteous for the sake of the unrighteous" (1 Peter 3:18 NAB).

It is finished! There is nothing we can add to what took place on Calvary. "For by grace you have been saved through faith, and this is not from you; it is the gift of God; it is not from works, so no one may boast" (Eph 2:8–9 NAB).

The moment when Jesus died on the cross, there was an earthquake. "The veil of the sanctuary was torn in two from top to bottom" (Mark 15:38 NAB).

The barrier vanished. Some scholars say that veil was about a foot thick made of fabric. An earthquake alone would not be able to rip it. It was God showing the Jews and the world it was no longer necessary. Ordinary men can now enter into the presence of God through Jesus Christ. "Therefore, since we have a great high priest who has passed through the heavens, Jesus, the Son of God, let us hold fast to our confession" (Hebrews 4:14 NAB).

I used to pray to different saints depending on the situation. Then I read: "For there is one God. There is also one mediator between God and the human race, Christ Jesus, himself human, who gave himself as ransom for all" (1Tim 2:5–6 NAB).

Okay, here's the big one. Don't get angry with me, just read it. Think about it, but most of all, pray about it. If Jesus is the one mediator, there can't even be two. Where does that leave Mary? Well, God used her in a powerful way to bring the Savior into the world. How's that? In Luke, Mary says, "…my spirit rejoices in God my Savior" (Luke 1:47 NAB).

Now, if she were without sin why would she need a Savior? Jesus had plenty of opportunities to teach us to pray to his mother Mary if that was his will. Instead, in Luke we read, "As Jesus was saying these things, a woman in the crowd called out, 'Blessed is the womb that carried you, and the breasts at which you nursed.'

He replied, 'Rather, blessed are those who hear the word of God and observe it'" (Luke 11:27–28, NAB).

This would have been a perfect time to say we should pray to Mary. He didn't. When the disciples asked Jesus, "Lord, teach us to pray," Jesus gave us the model that we call the Lord's Prayer. Who do we pray to?

"Our Father in heaven, hallowed be your name...." (Matthew 6:9, NAB).

I grew up believing that praying to Mary was like asking your mom so she would talk to your dad to pave the way. However, the Bible says, "Your Father knows what you need before you ask him" (Matthew 6:8, NAB).

As far as praying to saints, the apostle, Paul, refers to the believers in Christ as "holy ones," often translated as "saints."

We have *one* intercessor, Jesus Christ.

THE BENEDICTION

In Romans, we read, "All have sinned and are deprived the glory of God." (Romans 3:23, NAB). It doesn't say, "*Some* have sinned." Verse twenty-four continues, "They are justified freely by His grace through the redemption in Christ Jesus" (Romans 3:24, NAB).

The word *justified* can be thought of as "just as if I'd never sinned." Jesus was without sin, however, says Hebrews 4:15. Everybody born from the seed of Adam is born with a sinful nature. I learned it as original sin. I used to think that man was basically good. Then I had kids. What's the first word they learn? "No!"

The sinful nature shows its ugly head pretty early in life. Jesus was the *only* one without this sinful nature since the seed was from the Holy Spirit.

Now what? If you know you are saved, born again, and will spend eternity in heaven with Jesus and believe God has you serving in the Catholic Church, that's where you need to be. If you aren't sure where you're spending eternity, take care of that right now.

Pray something like this: *"Lord, I am a sinner, forgive me God. I turn from my sins and turn to you. Thank you for sending Jesus to die in my place and paying the price for my sin. Come into my heart and life and make me a new creation. I receive you as my savior and Lord.*

Amen."

If you've prayed this for the first time, tell someone. You probably know the person who has been praying for you. Get into God's Word. It is our instruction manual for life. Join a group of believers, other Christ followers, where you can serve and grow in the knowledge of our Lord. Tell others of the grace of God. You will never be the same!

PHOTO SECTION

5th Grade at St. Rose School

Easter 1958

A rare family photo, taken while I was on leave in the Navy
(Back row left to right) Mark, Ed, Lenore, Margaret, Phil and Joe (Front row left to right) Allen, Glenn, Anne and Rita

Playing for a Navy Wedding, base chapel, Newport Rhode Island 1973

August 19, 1978 Our Wedding,
Ridgewood United Methodist Church, Parma, OH

"Yesterday, Today and Forever" Andy Polakovs,
Ed Rothacker & Tom Henderson

Ship's Band "Damn Right" playing for USS Milwaukee AOR2 Reunion in Cleveland, OH July 2002

Members left to right: Joe Perino, Lenny Gatto, Roy Howell, Ed Rothacker, Gino Gallo, Bud McGovern and Floyd Shaw